V: AN ANTHOLOGY OF POETRY
Copyright © 2019 Respective Writers
All rights reserved. No part of this book may be used or reproduced in any manner whatsoever without written permission from the author, except in the case of credited epigraphs or brief quotations embedded in articles or reviews.

pictureshowpress.net

Cover image: Shchr, istockphoto.com

FIRST EDITION

ISBN-13: 978-1-7324144-4-0
ISBN-10: 1-7324144-4-0

V

An Anthology of Poetry

Picture Show Press

Contents

1	Behind the Velvet Curtain
3	misandry
4	Vajayjay
5	2 Nudes and a Cat
6	Emily Dickinson's Striptease
8	Water Cooler Gossip in the Animal Kingdom
9	She was vehement that she was a virgin
10	The gun on the nightstand
11	Thoughts While Thinking About What They're Talking About on TV About the Confirmation of an Alleged Drunken Attempted Rapist Jock for Supreme Court Justice of the United States of America
12	"V" is for Victim
14	The Streetwise Barbarian
15	Late Night Date
17	Vladimir
19	The Red Riding Hood Hearings
20	Pyre
21	Headmistress
24	Vixen
25	Moon
26	I pay tax to your grin
27	The Lovers Are Hungry
29	Mother Nature
30	Let Me Be Your Mirror
31	Scrabble
32	Heavy Weight, Clear Vinyl Shower Curtain ☆☆☆☆☆
33	Taken, Given
34	Flimsy veil
35	Variations of V
36	Pas de Deux
38	Blue Velvet
39	Viagra
40	The Birthday

42	*Shampoo*, Starring Warren Beatty, 1975
43	Ingénue
44	Lemon Drops
45	To All The Mothers Whose Sons I've Fucked
47	At Parties
48	no leatherette
49	Dear Nordstrom
50	I Could Taste the Scent
51	Street Artist, Melrose Avenue, Los Angeles, California
52	Ukelady Songbook
53	Walking Past the Whiskey A Go-Go, Los Angeles, California
54	The Two Coolest Chicks
56	Eternal Poet
57	Twenty Days, Indoors
59	Violent Green Synthesis
60	Finding the Tape
62	48 Steps
64	To My Piriformis
65	Chichi
66	Velvet Pipe Tobacco
67	Vehemently Voracious
68	Class
69	If I Were A Graffiti Artist?
70	Sharcas
71	Apology to the Palm Trees
72	The Perishables
73	We Tell Our Own Stories

Foreword

Why did I choose this letter as a "theme" for an anthology? It's pretty simple, actually: I like the way "V" sounds; I like the shape and feel of it in my mouth.

One night after a poetry reading at the dA Center for the Arts in Pomona, CA, a bunch of us went to get dinner (that's too formal — drinks? French fries? A drinkable creamsicle?). I was lucky enough to take part in a conversation about lyric poetry with the poets, Lloyd David Aquino and Michaelsun Stonesweat Knapp. At one point, I asked Michaelsun about a workshop he had taught one year during Mt. SAC Writers' Weekend, and I was so inspired that I had to take out my phone and make some notes. In my notes is this line: "If you find a sound you like, keep making it — Poetry according to Lloyd and Michaelsun."

Velvet, vulva, vixen, villain, vinyl, veil, voltage... are just some of the pleasing sounds you will find in this anthology.

My advice? Read it cover to cover. And read it out loud.

— Shannon, editor

Behind the Velvet Curtain | Aruni Wijesinghe

derived from the Latin for
wrapper, or covering
plural *vulvas* or *vulvae*

majora and *minora*
words sometimes assigned to
constellations

nested ballet slippers come
in graduated sizes
shades of blush and bashful

veiled antechamber
room to receive
invited and invader alike

visitors both animal and mechanical
of variable voltage
admitted with pleasure

unlike the Great and Powerful Oz
pay great attention to
the She behind the curtain

shy oyster gapes to reveal
her one treasure,
a single dark pearl

vixen and Victorian alike
entertain callers in this vestibule
ATM — Automated Titillation Machine

channel to communicate
one world to another,

thighs a clasp to restrict commerce

portal to
an interior universe —
not all gatekeepers are men

misandry | Kitty Anarchy

i asked a
man to
give me
a sentence
with *vulva*
in it

he didn't
even know
what the word
meant.

Vajayjay | Donna Hilbert

Everyone calls it vajayjay
now, you know, *down there*.
I read this in the *New York Times*.
Oprah says it.
Steinem has weighed in
hoping it contains the nervy bits
the real V-word ignores.
Me, I love the childhood name
taught by Mom and Mimi:
Whatsa-doodle-dandy!
Big happy word
that rhymes with candy.

2 Nudes and a Cat | Adrian Ernesto Cepeda

From a 1903 painting by Pablo Picasso

Canvas of fingers
reaching closer
while licking and tasting
her hunger, feeling her
vulva pleasure from her favorite
soft place. Watching, the pussy
cat is waiting, eyes closed
as her hips spreading hymns
when she purrs louder, signals
her one softest kitty, hardly ignored,
loudly she implores him to go
deeper, feeling inspired, he branches
through her curliest furs, rediscovering
lips gushing her delicious fountains,
hungering for something sweeter,
softly he licks up her frosting
like cake; spooning with desire —
he loves to savor her flavors
while blushing her most colorful face.

Emily Dickinson's Striptease | Kathryn McMurray

Every night, at the age of nineteen,
Emily Dickinson performed a solitary striptease.
Her velveteen budding breasts jiggling in the moonlight.
Picture her as she wiggles and squats,
legs apart, creamy peach cheeks spread enough
to let her ruddy earthish parts peek out.

She touches herself, often, nightly.
She thinks about this throughout the day;
even when her father's perverted geezer
friends come for tea and talk.
Especially then, twisting that clean, young
neck against the itch of the lace collar,
crossing her legs once, twice at the tickle of wetness.

What if, at the end of Emily Dickinson's naked
moonlight dance, she tiptoed secretly across
the sharp, cold hardwood floors
padding across the rug to the feather bed,
falling there softly?
Picture her then. She begins to touch,
a bit faster, and slower, then faster,
her consumptive little chest
wheezing tiny birdy breaths
with each finger twitch.
This goes on, and then...

In her mind, she suddenly imagines God.
Not a face, not God as some man from her life,
but the mistiness, the fog of God
closing in, closing in, the divine rush of Him
overtaking her like he seizes a church
woman speaking tongues,
her arms jerking just like that,

just   like   that
and in the last flail
she sees on her ceiling
as the Sistine Chapel,
that finger reaching out
not to Adam,
but between her legs.

Water Cooler Gossip in the Animal Kingdom | Aruni Wijesinghe

Are the lines
"The quick brown fox
jumped over
the lazy dog"
merely a simple typing exercise
to teach keyboard fluency?

Or is this a coded message
to warn women of color
in the secretarial pool
to dodge the advances of
their white bosses?

cautionary tale of
office politics

Can brown girls
in high-rise buildings
ever be complacent
about their precarious roles
in the executive suite?

How quick does a fox need to be
leaping over cubicle partitions,
darting through the copy room doorway?

Is the dog lazy
or feigning languor to trap
vixen prey?

lay in wait,
listen for the echo of
clicking heels
retreating down office corridors

untitled | Betsy Mars

She was vehement that she was a virgin
as she lay in a sticky sprawl
upon his vinyl divan.

His eyes virulent behind a veil
of violent desire. The electricity
between them, the surge in voltage
short-circuited his cognitive control.

He wound the wire around her wrists,
bound by the conviction
that she was a vixen
and he was no villain.

He felt the velvet groove of her vulva,
thrust aside any traces of virtue,
and in the voraciousness of victory,
hoped in vain that she would not be vindictive.

The gun on the nightstand | Holly Pelesky

I didn't lose my virginity
as much as I surrendered it.
The gun on the nightstand
whispered to me through its
cold barrel, *stay afraid* so I
lay still, blood wet beneath
me, staining his sheets, soaking
the air in a coppery sour, stitching
my mouth into silence, keeping my
feet from my shoes.

Thoughts While Thinking About What They're Talking About on TV About the Confirmation of an Alleged Drunken Attempted Rapist Jock for Supreme Court Justice of the United States of America | Joan Jobe Smith

All my life I've thought about that cute freshman girl in
high school, one of the cutest, sweetest of them all, thin,
cute clothes, a long light brown pony tail and what
happened to her, those Varsity jocks what they did to her,
first the quarterback, the best looking dating her getting her
to put out or get out when he drove to make out in the
orange groves no one to hear her yell Help if she
hadn't been so scared and her voice so squeaky-young
and someone out there in the shadows and moonlight
and orange blossoms to hear her and then the next date
she dared say No to too scared to refuse him when he
brought along the fullbacks and a left end (who always
caught his touchdown passes) and soon the jocks told
other jocks and what She Did was known by all who knew
the jocks and her mother, a WW2 widow rearing her daughter
all alone found out and moved away to another town and school.
Don't remember that cute girl's name as I imagine her and her
mother in a covered wagon gitty-upping lickity-splitting over
rocky hills and dusty dales, masked bandits shooting at the two
damsels in distress's sunbonnets and later that quarterback (who'd
get a scholarship to a good U and help win a Rose Bowl) came to
see me, home alone, the screen door unhooked and walked right
in without knocking woo'd me a minute before he reached like
Dracula for my neck and the phone rang so he stopped and it
was my father calling so the famous jock ran out the door.
Had I told my Texas daddy, he'd've shot that jock's ears off
or between the eyes making my getaway all much worse than
it was because even when we girls, and boys, too, are saved,
we're shamed, named the villains. Now my father's dead 52
years, the jock — whose name I never forgot nor his sandpapery
fingertips bruising my 16-year-old throat — and that cute girl are
very old and gray and today I think about them and what the hell
they are thinking about what they're talking about today on tv....

"V" is for Victim | LeAnne Hunt

Vindictive is a label for women
who come forward
       to speak a man's good name
          in their dirty mouths.
Women's silence is the veil
      men hide behind,
but whispers about what she wore,
      what she drank,
          why was she there
follow in her wake.
Victoria's Secret is worn against skin
      to be passed around.
Why a woman didn't report is the iron fist
in a man's velvet glove.
If she does, who believes her?
He said versus she said and she said
      and she said and she said,
the record is scratched vinyl spinning,
2018 and 1991
round and round.
Cannot educate a disbeliever
in statistics.
Comedy requires a punchline
and politics a poll.
Women's lives are too shrill in conversation,
so men cover their mouths
      for their own good.
We say vagina when we mean vulva —
lips are meant to be kept shut.
Men are stronger, and women too emotional —
      hysterical, says Ben Sasse.
But boys will be boys.
They cannot help it.
It is unfair to keep a good man down

           for holding a woman down on a bed.
A denial always trumps an accusation.
Women tend to walk into walls
and hit their heads on glass ceilings.
Was she a virgin?
           As if innocence were any kind of shield.
Virginity is defined by a lack of penetration
though 75% of women cannot orgasm from intercourse.
Consent and clitoris are synonyms for some men —
concepts to ignore.
No means yes, and yes means anal.
If it is going to happen, ladies,
just lie back and enjoy it,
           women are told.
A child by rape is God's gift
           without return.
But women cannot all be Mary
           unless Magdalene.
Why vehemently deny God's will
           or villainize men for 20 minutes of action?
Let a man's word fill you.
Why ruin a man's whole future for one or many mistakes?
Let the past lie
like women and their bodies below men.

The Streetwise Barbarian | Wendy Rainey

This is for the pit bull who clamped his jaws around my dog's throat
as we walked down my street on a sunny Tuesday afternoon.
And for the junkie from the halfway house who startled me
by wielding a screwdriver in my face
as I emptied the trash in my pajamas.
And the dude at Vons who crashed his cart into mine,
chatted me up, then appeared from behind
as I loaded my trunk with groceries.
Yes, come follow me out to my car in the underground parking lot.
I have something I want to show you in the back seat.
Let's party, just you, me, and my new toy.
I'll do crazy ass things to your body you'll never forget.
I'll make you scream like a bitch in heat.
My new toy has 65 million volts of FUCK YOU.
After I shock you three or four times
you'll lose all control of your bowels,
shitting your pants.
At which point I'll take the spiked end of my new toy
and spend the next five minutes tenderizing your meat.
When you come to, I will shine the strobe in your eyes
and push the little red button that delivers an earsplitting siren.
After several rounds of that you'll collapse onto the concrete,
begging for your mommy.
And I'll do it all with one hand because I'll need the other one free
to livestream it on my smartphone, of course.

Late Night Date | Thomas R. Thomas

you can see
the swing
in her hips

in the toe
impressions
in the wet
swampy grass

the heels
from her
black high heels
barely stabbing
the soil

she stands still
and straight

as straight
as her curves
will allow

her tall frame
towering above
the mound of
earth at
her feet

the mound of
earth seems
to shimmer
and shake

a closer look

reveals a
host of
vermin
crawling and
creeping over
the body

she stabs
the eye
socket
with her
knife

pulling out
a squirmy
creeper

then lays
the point
on her
tongue

Vladimir | Tamara Madison

Your other names:
Volodya, Vova —
names for mothers
and lovers to use.
How could either of these
apply to you?
Vanity has a home in your bared,
and hairless chest.
Venom, your secret weapon
Victor, your alter ego
Vlast — power — the root
of your name
and so you have it,
expert in its use.
Your whole life has led to this:
eyes that cut through the fog
in others' minds,
raptor eyes that hunt defenses,
laser through them to seek
the soft mouse
as it busies with its life.
The weakest ones believe
they've seen a soul
in your glacial eyes, imagine
the human in you and not
the snapper of bones
thrower from windows
wringer of necks
owner of all the ways
a man can make other men kill.
Vladimir
I know who you are.
Come to my house to guest,
as your people say.

Come to my house alone.
I will let my dog greet you
and do as he must.
You can kill me later.

The Red Riding Hood Hearings | Aruni Wijesinghe

Cast her in her true role:
villain, complete with velvet cape.
She played the victim, while he was
a sheep in wolf's clothing.

What did she expect would happen,
skulking around the woods in a crimson dress,
just begging to be eaten by
some wayward carnivore?

Such a thinly-veiled seduction,
giving directions to Grandmother's house.
Stooping to pick flowers was
a clear solicitation.

It is a predator's nature
to eat grannies, and
the wizened bitch in the nightgown
had it coming.

Such shameless flirtation with
all the questions of big ears, big eyes —
but the line about the teeth
was transparent invitation on her part.

Little Red Riding Hood
was more vixen than virgin,
a vindictive slut who compelled the woodsman
to gut a defenseless, crossdressing dog.

Couldn't she see it was all
just a big misunderstanding?
There was no record of premeditation
referenced in the wolf's carefully kept journal.

Pyre | Terry Ann Wright

after Mark Bibbins

I swore I wouldn't write about this anymore, my
accusations and apologies to you, self-declared doppelganger —

my heart, self, recoiled and refused your line; the lie climbs
higher and higher on the pyre. You made that up

for reasons I don't know, but I know that out
of all your veiled lies, this one somehow stings, of

all of them, the most. We are not the same person. The
calling on me as your other — me as your lake

monster, your twin, your friend, your ghost, and
above all, you — shutters my soul. Making me into

your darkness so you can be light. Making me into a
ghost so you can live. Making me an abyss, you a constellation.

Headmistress | Dania Ayah Alkhouli a.k.a. Lady Narrator

I did it, I texted him
Apparently 37 hours of threatening myself not to
failed against the Nike representative living somewhere inside me
    that said,
"Just do it!"
I broke an essential rule of the game but
I never play by the rules anyway, right?
Strike that
I never play
I refuse to
Since when did our hearts become toys to be played with?
And while your charming fingers claim to know their way around,
they are not welcome to tug at my heartstrings
Those are not chords on your instrument to be played

I am a woman
A woman in all her female formation and glory
who still somehow craves your everything
after another night of your nothing

When you're tipsy
you call me "Baby" and tell me I have game for days
I don't know whether to be utterly flattered or horrendously
    offended although,
when you're grabbing my waist and we're breathing each other,
I tell myself it's unmistakable flattery

But when you're sober,
I'm softly stroked by those charming fingers and
you call me intelligent and sexy

They say a drunk man's actions are a sober man's thoughts but
that makes me question even more whether I should be
flattered or offended

and I can't quite pin point where on that spectrum you lie
All I know is that you lie
and that everything around us vanishes when your ravishing hazel
    eyes fixate on mine
I thought only those in love are this good at eye contact?
Or are you just this good at this game?

Don't underestimate my capabilities though
You said my innocence never worked on you and yet, it has
You have no idea what can become of a woman —
born again from trauma
A phoenix birthed from the fire
The fire where she found herself thrust at the forefronts of learning
    the art of sex
as artillery
Because while the first man used it as a weapon against her,
she learned to use it as a shield against him

The pros and cons to being a survivor, I guess
You become both darker and lighter at the same time

Overnight I went from a virgin to the master in sexual artistry
Wearing the role of scandalous seductress like rosary beads around
    my neck,
calling out for salvation
Drinking the blood of a man who would never be my savior
Praying for the crucifixion to finally come

It never did and so instead
I stitched together a veil of darkness from my ashes
Slipped into it like that black lace I know calls to you
I leave behind perfect stiletto imprints no matter where I go
An irresistibly delicious trail of breadcrumbs you can't help but swallow
and that's why you're still here

We have each other exactly where we want the other to be
and I haven't even shown you the half of what I can do

So baby, boast all you want about the full decade and a half you
    have on me in years,
the magnificent student you are of the female form, but at the end
    of the day,
while you are just a student of the female form,
I *am* the female form
with so much more to teach you than you can handle

So yeah, I texted him
and there are no regrets because in the end this is not a game,
this is education
And he will never find another woman better equipped
to educate him

Vixen | Holly Pelesky

It isn't hard to find a lover,
only to keep one.

Once he says *I love you*,
I smile, hold his hand, drop
my head into the dip
of his shoulder.

Never do I love him back.

I zip into his adoration, let it
cradle me for awhile.
Let it hold me in tight, warm
against its bosom, as if I belong
somewhere.

Then,
I drop out — when
the man who's confusing me with love
smells like sweat again, no longer
sweet like infatuation.

This is how I leave them: goose bumped,
shaky, an unlit cigarette between clenched teeth,
wondering why I can't give love like a smile.

Moon | Terry Ann Wright

I'm all in, you say, and so am I.
I promise you I'm not going anywhere

though I keep my fingers crossed
behind my back. If I leave,

I'm leaving for good, and it will be
in spite of you, not because.

I know how little comfort that offers
and so I don't offer it at all.

I promise to try, is what I whisper
when I know you can't hear.

I don't know how to be different.
The biggest villain is my own heart.

I pay tax to your grin | Sarah Thursday

claim its design as my quaking place
it's all I have left of me
under the heel of my boot
I forget them
that they ever shared
the core temperature of my pulse
when your pocket is full of switchblades
the net I cast around you
is no more than broken threads
we, poised for science's last stand
killing swagger by each precise shiver
drug down her knobby spine
it was a cruel stunt
even for vindictive types
the reverse of him sat soup-can-still
it takes practice to be as agreeable
as they need us to be
be we do
until he smolders
quiet as a molten piano

The Lovers Are Hungry | Terry Ann Wright

She drinks too much, but being a poet, it's okay.
He fights too much, but he'd rather punch the jerk in the bar
than think about going home alone, so it's okay.

In this age they barely connect:
her phone refuses to call his country,
his runs out the battery, the flurries of missives
crossing a 15-hour time difference means

a poem gets lost, a question goes unanswered.

Some things can't be put into words, he says,
and it comforts them both for now,
but when they can't touch each other, words are all they have.

Some evenings are spent separating their emotions.

Marbles fall and clack: the glassy bright swirls of color
fool their friends, themselves, each other:
I'm fine, how are you, wasn't that fun, lunch tomorrow?

but

I miss him and
I can't bear to be apart from you one more day and
come home, come home

bump and roll into the velvet bag of night.

She believes she can feel him walk down the hallway to her,
turns her head, waits for the caress of his hand.

Come over, he says on the phone. *Come over right now.*

Go to sleep, she says, *and I'll crawl into the bed
while you're dreaming. You'll wake up and I'll be there.*

The chasm between them warps and waxes.

He smokes and smokes and lies and lies.

In the brightest sunlight he closes the blackout drapes
and opens the air conditioner and crawls between
the cool white sheets where he burns and burns.

Mother Nature | Dania Ayah Alkhouli a.k.a. Lady Narrator

The vindictive silence that accompanies her when another man leaves
almost makes her nostalgic for the howling wolves they once gave
 birth to inside her.
Every passing year she questions if settling really is all that bad?
Like vinyl, spinning,
never skipping a beat.
Systematic and predictable.
She doesn't have to settle for a *bad* man. She can settle for what's
 safe. What's present.
What'll keep her company under those full moons.
But she's been saying *what* — *what* will keep her company — not *who*.
Maybe that's the problem with settling.

You can only hear, "You deserve better," so many times before it
 becomes a myth.
An urban legend whispered over campfires about the woman
who once lived
with spirit.
She was never the right amount though.
Always too much
or never enough.

Let Me Be Your Mirror | Adrian Ernesto Cepeda

I will show every inch
of your skin, so soft I love
to expose as you seductively
lift-up your slightly undersized
tee's, showing your midriff,
tummy grins your belly
button all I display my mirror
length. Let me be your sight,
look beyond any glimpse you
may have once despised — I will
shine, your softest knees, while
flashing your body, a work
of art a master-pièce with no
résistance, my tender bella
you will always be a canvas
in these eyes already there
picturing your tastiest peachy
backside arching delicately
perking flirty décolletage peeking
through wondrously nippling
thunder focusing all you, as
my mirror shrines you stunningly
framed. You will always shine
streaking as my looking glass
reflects every underground
velvety pose, proudly revealing
while worshiping you
my favorite vision always
glowing ravishingly untamed.

Thank you @dylanwk

Scrabble | John Grey

We're playing Scrabble
at the kitchen table.
I move tiles around,
first with my mind,
then my fingers.

Gale sits opposite,
I associate cricket chirp,
traffic noise,
a distant dog bark,
with her concentration.

We seldom play games,
rarely place ourselves
in opposition to each other.

Usually we're like
words that form themselves
without intervention.
Not these consonant and vowels
we've dealt ourselves
that resist any combination
beyond a few meager points.

In life, we're triple letters scores,
triple words even,
not these modest efforts
like "fly" and "was" and "did"
slowly filling up the board.

By the time we're done,
one of us will have won.
I prefer it
when we start out winning.

Heavy Weight, Clear Vinyl Shower Curtain
☆ ☆ ☆ ☆ ☆ | Alexis Rhone Fancher

I disturb your shower, fresh towels my excuse
to watch you stand beneath the spray,

water pouring off your hair, trickling down
your shoulders, beading your studly chest.

Fresh towels, the excuse for my eyes to linger
at your soaped-up cock, stiff in your hand.

I drop the towels, pull off my dress,
press myself into the vinyl, cool to the touch.

An inspired purchase, I think.

You reach for my breasts, slather your face between
the fogged, wet vinyl and me, mouth my nipples,

grip your cock harder, faster.

I reach between my legs for my clit,
finger myself to match your pace,
your hand a blur.

When your blue eyes close, I pull my fingers from inside me,
push aside the curtain, slide them into your mouth
watch you lick your lips, grin.

Sometimes, we see right through each other.

Tomorrow I'll give the shower curtain a 5-star Amazon review,
as the seller, a mom and pop in Idaho, requested,
if I'm satisfied.

Taken, Given | Natalie L. Peterkin

It's astonishing how little i remember.

It must have been summer.
The cramped, two-bedroom apartment
was empty. His mom worked at
Jack-in-the-Box and Corner Bakery
to keep a roof over their heads
and a stained beige carpet beneath their feet.
We kissed as only teenagers do
all teeth, tongue, and desperation.
Our clanging mouths had something to prove:
we were adults, capable of pleasure,
deserving of love. When he asked if i wanted
to have sex, my mind went blank, like i was
counting the space between molecules, the
nanoseconds separating my lips from the response they'd soon utter.

Being a virgin was an obstacle, an abstraction of womanhood
separating me from the adult knowledge
of what made fucking so sacred.
i shouldn't know, but i wanted to.
It had very little to do with him
even less to do with his penis
and almost nothing to do with the way
it hurt
then felt good
then hurt again.
i don't remember if we were in love.
Perhaps i thought we were.
i don't remember if we fumbled like newborn calves
i'm sure we did.
i do remember it was evening
and his window was facing east.
i felt the sunset inside of me
without ever looking outside.

Flimsy veil | Holly Pelesky

My skirt splayed
around my thighs,
over my ass:
a flimsy veil.

We both knew
I would reveal,
knew how he would
fill me, and then
how he wouldn't.

I looked
down into his eyes,
saw only want and
forgot how the
story
ends.

He lifted
my veil,
light and airy
as if
it had never
been there.

Variations of V | Brian Harman

She sucked me like a quantum vacuum.
I invaded her like an 80s alien-lizard
TV miniseries;
intentions of love
lacking verisimilitude,
when opening up and revealing
becomes invention,
ever so slowly, so lonely,
and it's over like a mirrored casket burial,
to move on, across stepping stones of tombs,
divinity in a dark cloud
waiting for velocity's return,
to be alive
without envy, to be back
craving, scratching, grasping
the vernacular of bedded passion,
oh yes, oh god, oh fuck — into the vortex,
the ventriloquistic heart,
the vertical spread,
the voluptuous
void.

Pas de Deux | Alexis Rhone Fancher

1. She said: *Tell me one thing that doesn't end badly?*

2. I wanted her ruffled tutu and toe shoes,
pink satin ribbons latticed up my legs like body armor.

She knew I avoided mirrors, reflecting pools.
What, she asked, *do you dislike about your face?*

3. Hers was a thoughtless beauty,
while I worked hard for everything,

danced my body into submission,
those endless practice hours at the *barre,*
legs turned out, toes pointing, pointing.

4. *La laisse tomber,* she said, when I leapt,
head-first into her arms. She let me fall.

5. I dreamed a solo, spotlight, applause,
not tucked in the corps de ballet.

She, too, dreamed prima ballerina. On stage,
her wicked tour jetés just missed my face.

6. *A dancer in love with anyone but herself
is called an understudy,*
she laughed when I asked her to choose.

That night, I arabesqued right through her;
she tasted jealousy for the first time.

7. She became a self-fulfilling prophecy,
out till dawn, sex-soaked, sweaty with another,
less ambitious girl's perfume. (See #1).

8. When I found the photos with my eyes x'ed out, I knew I would leave her.

My eyes – my one good feature.

Blue Velvet | Curtis Hayes

we walked out of a mostly empty
shopping mall theater
and filtered into the exiting crowd
from the blockbuster action film
that had been exploding through the wall
between us.
we were nearly to the car
before I looked at her and said,
"That may be the best film I've ever seen."
she was walking faster than me.
"What was it even about?"
"I'm not sure yet."
I opened the door for her
then climbed in behind the wheel.
I started the engine.
 "You don't think it was just weird
for the sake of being weird?" she asked.
traffic was backed up in the parking structure
there was ten minutes of ugly concrete
lit by a slow corkscrew of creeping taillights.

she was a nice girl, pretty and sweet.
she worked in an office
and I was fumbling clumsily through life.
she wanted to move in with me.
I made the turn out onto the boulevard.
she held my hand
as the streetlights flashed around us.
"I think it may be my favorite movie, ever."
I knew we wouldn't be together for long.

Viagra | Kevin Ridgeway

I took one of my father's prescription pills
and tried to reconcile with my wife one night.

She went to sleep and I had a boner even
I wanted to divorce as well once she ran away
from the two of us lonesome medicated
brainless fuck machines from hell.

The Birthday | Wendy Rainey

The last time I saw him
was on his ninety-third birthday.
He was in a hospital gown
and diapers.
She was in her diamonds and pearls,
stooped over him,
kissing his face,
leaving a trail of lipstick
on his cheeks and neck.
Her perfume,
which I had told her had gone bad
six months earlier,
wafted through the room.

There were flowers on the table
and birthday cards from his friends and relatives
who never came to visit him.
I wondered if he had told them
not to come,
or if they just didn't want to see him,
or perhaps it was a combination of both.
"Don't live to be ninety-three, kiddo.
The rule of thumb is
if you can't wipe your own ass anymore
then it's time to kick the bucket."

I set down the banana bread
I had baked for him
and some coffee from Starbuck's.
"Isn't this lovely?" she said,
her hand on mine.
"You've never just been a caregiver to us.
You're like family."
I smiled at her.
She took a sip of coffee
and squinted at me.

"Are you my niece?"
she asked a few moments later.
"No, I'm your caregiver."
"Oh, that's right,"
she took another sip of her coffee.
"What did you say your name was?"

As we ate the banana bread
and drank the coffee,
I noticed some travel brochures
scattered on his bed.
"Wake up in a new world,"
one of them said.
"Are you going somewhere?"
"I'm blowin' this joint, honey,"
he laughed.
"By this time tomorrow
I'll be home again,
floating on a raft in my pool.
I'm gonna have a cigar
in this hand
and a scotch on the rocks
in this hand," he chuckled.
"There'll be live jazz,
BBQ'd ribs,
bare-titted virgins…"

"Hey, I'm gonna go topless too!"
She kissed his forehead.
He reached for her.
"Darlin, you've been driving me crazy
for seventy-one years
and I've loved every bit of it."
I watched him give her hand a little squeeze.
She held on,
her fingers resting
between the I.V.
and his wedding ring.

Shampoo, Starring Warren Beatty, 1975 | Kareem Tayyar

Sometimes I still imagine a life
Like the one Warren Beatty has in this film:
Riding a motorcycle through the Los Angeles hills,
Romancing society women,
Fashion models,
Free-lovers,
Willing virgins,
And Julie Christie,
All the while with no greater stress on his mind
Than whether he can remember their names.
Of course it isn't much of a life.
Even on the eve of an election that will give
The country Richard Nixon,
Neither Beatty nor any of his girlfriends
Seem aware of any world beyond
The adult playgrounds of Beverly Hills
That they frequent.
Maybe that's why the daydreams never last long,
And I feel so guilty afterwards.

Ingénue | Donna Hilbert

She was a 1930's ingénue
scared spit-less before each interview
until her mother dribbled bourbon
into her breakfast tea
and then poured more
into a dainty flask.
"For the road," the mother said,
and strapped the flask to her thigh.
"You're prettier than the other girls,
smarter too," she said,
and sent her through the door
into her new life
as bit-part actress, vixen,
and the second most famous
model in Hollywood.

Lemon Drops | Kathryn McMurray

Her name was Sandie or Cindie or something.
She had big tits, I remember, and strawberry-blonde hair.
They bounced around, her tits, inside her brown turtleneck
when she plopped herself down on the white, tuck-and-roll
front seat of my dad's car. My mother's breasts, by now,
had drooped to her ribcage from breastfeeding three kids
in a row, before she was twenty-five.
Sandie or Mandie smiled brightly at me.
She said, *Hiya. I heard so much about you.*
Wanna lemon drop?
While she clicked her nails around in her purse,
searching for that tin of candies,
I wondered if my mom knew where I was,
if she knew that my dad was introducing me to strangers
with big breasts and long, red fingernails.

We were going to a movie: my dad, Mandie and I.
They giggled and teased each other.
Carlie liked country-western. My dad shoved
in an eight-track of The Flying Burrito Brothers,
and I slid around on the vinyl of the backseat,
sucking on my lemon drop with slit eyes,
while he showed off the pick-up on his accelerator.
She stroked his chops with her talons and he pounded out
beats on the steering wheel.

When we dropped Candie off she asked me,
Didja hava good time? Do ya wanta nother lemon drop?
She held the tin of powdered candy out in the palm of her hand.
Her long, red fingernails curled around the outside of the tin.
I heard my mother telling me for the millionth time:
Don't, under any circumstances, take candy from strangers.

To All The Mothers Whose Sons I've Fucked | Natalie L. Peterkin

My mother told me
Pay attention to how a man
treats his mother
because that's how
he'll treat you
a maxim I ignored
but has since crept back into my mind
gaining truth with age.
One day, I'll be the mother
my son's loves see
through the veil of him
never quite knowing me.

I.
We sat on the stoop for hours
as only teenagers and old folks do
and she yells out the window in Spanish
Throw some hot water on her
assuming I wouldn't understand.
I didn't. *What did she say about water?*
I ask my boyfriend, but he waves away my inquiry
before excusing himself inside.
To her, I was a nuisance
a feral cat in heat
yowling and rubbing its vulva
on her precious potted plant.

II.
I never met her, but she had his face —
a wide, gregarious smile and small, black eyes.
He wasn't handsome, and she wasn't pretty
but both of them were beautiful.
I wondered if she moved like he moved

with slow, calculated steps
if she, too, woke every morning
with dreams caught in her scraggly hair
if, like him, she withheld affection
as a silent, vindictive punishment
I couldn't seem to avoid.

III.
Her house had white, fluffy carpet.
I couldn't imagine the anxiety
that went into keeping it clean.
There was a heated pool
three extra rooms to escape into
a dining room nobody ate in
and dustless family pictures in the hallways.
I drove there drunk one night.
My boyfriend wasn't even home but
I rang the doorbell until she answered
bleary-eyed and confused in a pink bathrobe.
I smelled like a disparaging combination
of whiskey and regret, so she let me pass out in his bed.
I woke up thinking she would hate me now
or at least be suspicious, but she never mentioned it.
She let some piss-drunk vixen treat her house like a hotel
and in my eyes, she became a fool.

IV.
She was blindingly beautiful with velvet black hair
and crooked teeth which nonetheless crafted a smile
so pleasing to look at. She graded Spanish tests
over a glass of Sangria at a Mexican buffet in Baldwin Park
narrating with small comments: *Oh, not quite. Good. Nope.*
She was nothing like her son: charming, level-headed, gracious.
He was fidgeting with his straw, making sarcastic observations
about the restaurant's lackluster horchata when I told him
You need to be more like your mother.

At Parties | Donna Hilbert

Mary P. would go into the bedroom
take off all her clothes,
put on someone else's fur coat,
sashay her way through the crowd.
Even drunk, she must have felt the voltage —
all that white flesh, naked under mink.

no leatherette | Kitty Anarchy

going to
Perversions
dressed
in my
vinyl outfit.
there is a
subtle sound
it makes
when you
walk and
it is
surprisingly
forgiving.

everyone is
fierce in vinyl.

Dear Nordstrom | Alexis Rhone Fancher

Dear Nordstrom,

I'm returning the red velvet party dress I bought for M.'s birthday, unworn. Yes, it hugs my ass, and the fine lace inset exploits my breasts, and although it makes me feel like a vixen, the unexpected break up with my intended (for reasons I don't want to get into except to say I most certainly *am* divorced from my 3rd husband) makes the dress irrelevant. Anyway, maybe it's best I didn't go to the party, because my friend Bambi says I'd have been way overdressed — that she was the only one in a frock, because this, after all, is California. *People showed up dressed like they were going to the laundromat or the movies!* she said, forever an East Coast girl. Her high heels sank into the soggy lawn of the backyard where refreshments were served. I could have been a refreshment myself, in red velvet, but I'd rather be naked and watching a movie. Eating red velvet cake. Or fucking. Look, if I had a nickel for every party I didn't attend I'd still bring back the dress. Nordstrom, your return policy is legendary. The tag, like my heart, is still attached.

Faithfully Yours,
A

I Could Taste the Scent | Adrian Ernesto Cepeda

Hints of cigarette smoke
hidden as the aura of tobacco
reigned within the strands
in her long curly purple
unwashed hair. I would never
have guessed she would light
up. Maybe it's her secret
craving, her mister never
sniffs out. On her longest
trips, this secret fire is the one
treat she gifts herself, buying
one pack, burying it deep inside
her purse, along with the purple
Bic lighter or the one perfect
match, the striking sound always
excites her like the touch of her

smokiest paramour. She loves
the flavor as his addicting
smoke rises and discreetly
touches her lips, inhaling
each gust like an invisible
kiss that only she knows
about. Maybe his nicotine air
is the one passion she has left,
keeping his smoke veiled
underneath Altoids mints,
TheraBreath tablets and ultra
Sensodyne ProNamel toothpaste
to cover the kiss, she longs
to taste his flame and reignites
his flavor, in the dark she desires
each puff, it's his mist alone
she covets inside her most
secret breath.

Street Artist, Melrose Avenue, Los Angeles, California | Kareem Tayyar

The young woman in velvet pants stands before the wall,
A large paintbrush in her hand,

Creating a pair of wings for the angel
She has brought into the world.

I haven't prayed in weeks.

But now I find myself whispering
A small grace as she adds color
To the feathers,

Blessed that this red light is taking
So long to turn green.

Ukelady Songbook | Kevin Ridgeway

she kissed me from across the room
the vixen with the long smooth legs
playing her ukulele like a novelty out
of a quaint gift shop, her song book
posted to my wall for months due
to my unrequited drunken Northern
New England summer back road
make out point love for her, but
she ran away with the cooler kids
and left me behind to remember
the curls of her hair and the spark
of her mischievous smile, and how
she talked me down from a weed
and albuterol induced psychosis,
Mungo Jerry hacking away a song
I will always remember the sexy
girl in the mini skirt peddling me
into steamed heat that women
on ukuleles cover to do a sensual
number on all of my numerous
goose pimple memories.

Walking Past the Whiskey A Go-Go, Los Angeles, California | Kareem Tayyar

As a child I'd look for Belinda Carlisle everywhere:

Standing in front of Galco's Soda Shop,
Nursing a Dr. Pepper and sporting a neon miniskirt;

Roller-skating along the Venice Boardwalk in a red bikini,
Her head full of the hits that would own the radio the following year;

Thumbing through the vinyl stacks at the Tower Records on Sunset,
Looking for lost classics by Big Star and The Beach Boys.

I was six, seven years old,
Which meant I didn't know what love was.

I just knew that whatever Belinda was feeling in "Head Over Heels"
Was what I felt about her.

The Two Coolest Chicks | Curtis Hayes

sitting in my car near midnight
the end of another grueling day on set,
pushing lights
pulling power
going nowhere
and now waiting for my turn at a drive-thru speaker.
I try not to think too hard
about the mystery meat tacos
coming my way,
hoping that the late-shift
kid on the grill
doesn't read my mind
and spit on my tortillas.
I spin the radio dial,
stare at the taillights in front of me
and when the deejay finally shuts up
and the first familiar notes unwind
her voice
instantly
unravels the knots in my head.
Chrissie – the Pretender.
I flash back decades
to Kerry, my high school girlfriend
whose parents were never home
and me and Kerry would lay
on thick worn-out 70's shag carpet
in front of a big console record player
listening to that album over and over.
Kerry was the coolest chick at school,
she had the look and even better
the attitude.
next to her, the cheerleaders
and everyone else just looked silly.
and Chrissie,

with her black bangs, leather pants
and a voice that could cut glass
Precious
Brass in Pocket
Mystery Achievement
Talk of the Town.
no one on record could touch her.

I burned through a year with Kerry
cruising in her old Chevelle
through drive-in movies
2am taco stands
and teenage desire.
but the best was
listening to records
laying head to head on the shag
like Siamese Twins
until it was time
to get up and flip the vinyl.

I slide a few dollars into a tray
a bored kid behind bullet proof glass
slides back some change
I leave it
and head for
my darkened house
thinking about tomorrow's
5am alarm clock
and the time when I spent long afternoons
down in the shag
with Kerry and Chrissy
the two coolest chicks in the world.

Eternal Poet | Kevin Ridgeway

she hated AA
because of God
who was not
the eternal poet
she worshiped
beyond human
comprehension.
Joni Mitchell
ignited her words
from adolescent
vinyl escapes
and so did
Bob Dylan
who was a
prophet from
the same
northern
land she
was born into,
those rambling
gypsies
who danced
around all
expectations
but she was
too quiet
but then again,
I guess
the world
did not
deserve
what she
shared
with a
lucky
chosen
few.

Twenty Days, Indoors | Aldo Moreno

There is a voltage
that hangs around the house.

I feel it when I lay
bare backed on the carpet,

charting patterns
in the cottage ceiling.

It shows up unexpected,
a warm wind that rolls on

through a winter where
nothing else exists.

Too many days indoors
and I'm starting to lose sense.

The voltage picks me up,
whispers in my ear,

tells me there are things to do,
that a productive day is only a step

away. It breaks my heart to claim it.
It makes me want to clean,

and so I get to work scrubbing
the corners of the bathroom,

every detail of the oven,
its iron bars caked in carbon,

and when I finally look

behind the bed, expecting

a spider or the dust of a mite,
I find two five dollar bills,

a blue pen, and the sleeve
for a Miles Davis vinyl,

his face, his eyes
looking up to ask me

"where have *you* been?"
to which I have no answer.

Violent Green Synthesis | A. E. Sadeghipour

Aren't we all just living on an 80's vinyl?
hidden behind the techno synths
bodies undulating with
subhuman convulsive vibrations
if I was a color,
I would be electric green
and sometimes violet
Pretty
borderline offensive
dichotomy of auditory
pleasure visual pain
which attracts you?
pleasure/pain
I am violent green
on 80's vinyl
and god damnit
I will make you
feel something.

Finding the Tape | John Grey

At the bottom of the trunk,
amid yellow wedding dresses
and fluttering moths,
super 8 home movies,
I find an old reel to reel tape
marked with a felt pen – "Family."

The machine to play it
is quickly dusted,
plugged in
and cued up to the beginning
with a silent plea –
"Don't jam the gears."

I turn it on
and someone's speaking.
"I'm recording this."
Another person talks
but their words fade in and out.
The brown spool is doing its best
but it's flecked in places.
A loud whooping sound
suggests further damage.

Then someone says,
"Play something Clarence."
Clarence is my dead uncle,
though not so deceased
he can't blast a note or two
out of his beat-up saxophone.
"You're too close to the mike,"
the first voice complains.
I wonder if it's my father.
Sometimes I wonder if everything

unexplained, not quite clear,
so close, so distant,
is he.

For now, I'm the family archaeologist
unearthing the bones of voices,
the flesh of what they could do.
The reels, as ever, slowly spin.

48 Steps | Brian Robert Flynn

This morning, back and forth
and up and down,
I stepped the same old steps.

My wake up, take a shower,
brush my teeth,
get ready steps. Then I

took what to many
might seem like a million steps.
But it wasn't

a million steps,
it was more like
a few city miles of steps.

I savored my breakfast:
Biscuits and gravy, eggs,
potatoes, heavy

like a tire, like dinner.
Then the mettle to write this
coincided

with ideas of how
convenient one of those
digital step-counters

might be. But
what then would the point be,
but a recording of numerals?

Too precise,
too statistical. As in

if that's what I'm after,

then why not just count up
all the steps anyway
sans pedometer

instead of opting to comb hair
or tie shoelaces?
Forego

the art of
accounting for velvety
blue chicory coffeeweed

sprouting like vines
between winos slumbering
unfazed by the dawn.

Not to mention
heeding or beating
all the bloody red lights

and traffic signals.
I might die, and WTF
would the point of that be?

Just now I took
48 steps
to grab another cup of tea.

To My Piriformis | Donna Hilbert

O muscle shaped a bit like a pear
buried deep inside my cheeky rear,
I apologize for not knowing your name
prior to your recent bid for fame
clenching yourself so fisty-tight
that I can't climb a single flight
of stairs without crying stupidly in pain.
I've had to stop and ponder what villain
lies in wait — vindictive, un-named —
ever eager to insult, injure, maim.

Chichi | Kitty Anarchy

the cat *JOLTS!* onto the kitchen counter

delicately tippy toe ing

past the t.v and the remotes mismatched jewelry bottle of wine cup o' nail files cup o' pens hot sauces bags of chips napkins 2 liter glass Mexican soda bottles virgin mary pics prayer cards and charms the telephone notes combs massage ball roller massage cream ceramic cups at least 4 pairs of sunglasses face cream big container of salt keychains toaster oven & toaster the hot water kettle blender the coffee can sugar bowl etc.

lifting
front
paws
HIGH

s t r e t c h i n g back legs as needed
with laser-like precision

to get
to the open can
of cat food
by the sink.

without dropping

        a

            single

                  thing.

Velvet Pipe Tobacco | A.E. Sadeghipour

Velvet Pipe Tobacco
like a veranda's equinox
Contorting in Contusions
of ribbons

Lackluster
King Cluster
Corridors

indominable
incorrigible
chrysanthemums
flick
chrysanthemums
incorrigible
indominable

Corridors
Cluster King
Lackluster

ribbons of
Contusions in Contorting
veranda's equinox like a
Tobacco Pipe of Velvet

Vehemently Voracious | A. E. Sadeghipour

I am vehemently voracious
consuming everything
processor overloading
maintaining multiple functions
simultaneously starving
bursting
needing information input
output
constantly uploading,
downloading,
editing,
uploading,
downloading,
editing,
uploading,
downloading,
editing,
uploading,
downloading,
deleting,
deleting,
deleting,
deleting,
creating
storage
space
RAM drive
memory

Class | Sarah Thursday

I am not marker-stained fingers
I am not dry eraser streaks on a white board
Not gray-grubbed carpet
or under desk gum
I am not crumpled drafts
not frayed-edges curling
I am not soot smears from broken lead
Not worn book covers peeling
I am newly pulled tooth and bleeding gums
I am finished drafts,
words layered on eraser thin paper
I am zip-up sweater,
shorts too tight, finger smeared t-shirts
I am curls and sleek ponytails, gel-cracked hair standing
I am bitten nails, worn tennis shoes
and raised hand.

If I Were A Graffiti Artist? | Brian Robert Flynn

If I were a graffiti artist, I'd paint more red bricks
on top of already red bricks.

The subway cars, I'd shroud in dittoed,
silver-lined realism, in a repeating light
to echo easily and thoroughly
my own metallic reflection shining back.

The boulevard I'd re-swab in black-top black,
revirginizing its tarry notes amid
my re-paved jots of yellow light guiding exhaustively.
Yes, that's my lacquer re-glowing the dashes
to re-keep safe each car that passes.

To be sure, the city's fire engines
I'd re-slather fire engine red,
and I'd lovingly lionize the patrol cars
in their same old Hill Street blue.
"To Protect And To Serve,"
I'd squarely re-embolden, too.

And I'd comply if they told me to move along,
because I'd know that they know
there's nothing to see here.

Sharcas | K. Andrew Turner

Grandpa calls me a silly girl
when I watch the sun set.
I love the vibrant hues,
the transformation
from orange
        to red
                and purple
the painted vaults of the sky.

I watch the Gods lower the sun
and leach the vivid color
into homogenous, inky black.
Only pinpricks of light
that we call sharcas —
wandering flames.
I wish to wander with them,
dance in the velvet blanket,
but Grandpa calls me silly.

I am supposed to be strong
support our village
        by feeding them
        protecting them
I am told I should be
like my brother.

But all I want to do
is gaze into the ether
and leave these chains behind
and soar with the sharcas
forever free
forever free
no longer a silly girl
but a woman
burning bright
shedding hope in
eternal darkness.

Apology to the Palm Trees | Sarah Thursday

I called you false
branchless spindles
vindictive fronds
hung like heavy fingers
You are undefinable
how you ignore gravity
how you sink through earth
like veins in muscles
indistinguishable
you live in sky
like blue is bed
like wind is exhale
I thought you ugly
thought you pointless
until I saw defiance as purpose
how you live in narrow surface
so little displaced below
forgive me
for dismissing your relevance
for casting you vixen of Hollywood Boulevard
I'm sorry
we, villains of convention
should stand together

The Perishables | Brian Robert Flynn

To the Arm & Hammer baking soda
in the back of the refrigerator,
the sixty-watt incandescent bulb electrifies
a moment of resistance and acceptance
all at once.

Sunrise, a hand from heaven reaching
for a tomato-red bottle.
And look, she's dropped off something new.
"Is it soup?" Then quickly, her sun sets.

There are no plums in this icebox.
No butterflies, nothing fluttering past
to while by time. There is butter, though.
There's the ripened stench of onions, too,
lurking for me to kill.

A leftover roast sits frightened, tonight.
Here in the air-conditioned dark,
Arm & Hammer stifles the acrid odor,
an appeasement to the meathook in the sky
if she appears at the crack of dawn beneath
her veil of blinding light.

We Tell Our Own Stories | Dania Ayah Alkhouli a.k.a. Lady Narrator

If it's not yours,
can you really even talk about it?

Decades of hearing everyone else aimlessly try and narrate our story
Tell us who we are, who we should be, who we need to become
No one ever saw the pens in our hands
The vehement words on our tongues
The wildness of our souls

Our story was always ours to write — always will be
But since it's not yours, can you really even talk about it?

History.

Religion.

Race.

Culture.

Ethnicity.

Love.

If it's not yours, can you really even talk about it?

BIOS

Dania Ayah Alkhouli (a.k.a. Lady Narrator) is a Syrian American poet and author. At 19, she published her first book of poetry, *91 at 19*. Almost a decade later, she released her second, *Oceans & Flames*, a collection of poetry on her experience with, and survival of, domestic abuse. In 2012, she and her mother co-founded the nonprofit *A Country Called Syria*, a traveling exhibition that highlights the history, culture, and beauty of Syria.

Kitty Anarchy is an anarchafeminist, chicana womyn poet and short story writer. She listens to KPFK and NPR. She has 7 cats, her favorite being ChiChi and 2 dogs named Bandit and Nibbit. www.kittyanarchy.com

Adrian Ernesto Cepeda is the author of the poetry collection *Flashbacks & Verses... Becoming Attractions* from Unsolicited Press and the poetry chapbook *So Many Flowers, So Little Time* from Red Mare Press. Adrian is an LA Poet who has a BA from the University of Texas San Antonio and an MFA from Antioch University in Los Angeles where he lives with his wife and their cat Woody Gold. Connect with Adrian at: www.adrianernestocepeda.com

Alexis Rhone Fancher is published in *Best American Poetry 2016, Rattle, Hobart, Verse Daily, Plume, Tinderbox, Cleaver,* and elsewhere. Her books include: *How I Lost My Virginity to Michael Cohen..., State of Grace: The Joshua Elegies, Enter Here,* and *Junkie Wife.* Her photographs are published worldwide, including the covers of *Witness, Heyday,* and *Pithead Chapel,* and spreads in *River Styx* and *Chiron Review.* A multiple Pushcart Prize nominee, Alexis is poetry editor of *Cultural Weekly.*

Originally from the Mile High City, **Brian Robert Flynn** is presently breathing the fiction and poetry of Albuquerque, New Mexico. His writing can be found in *Clarion, Jelly Bucket, (b)OINK, Cease Cows, Hobart,* and the *Glasgow Review of Books.*

John Grey is an Australian poet, U.S. resident. Recent publications include: *The Homestead Review, Poetry East,* and *Columbia Review* with work upcoming in *Harpur Palate, The Hawaii Review,* and *North Dakota Quarterly.*

Brian Harman is from Yorba Linda, CA. He received his MFA in Creative Writing from Cal State University, Long Beach. He's an Aries, loves music, long walks; writes his poetry deep into the night. Some of his poems have appeared in *Chiron Review, Bank Heavy Press, Pearl,* and *Nerve Cowboy.* If you see him around, feel free to join him for a cup of coffee, craft beer, fine wine, or a shot of something good.

Curtis Hayes has worked in sawmills, greasy spoons, and as a grip, gaffer, and set builder in film productions. He's been a truck driver, a boat rigger, a print journalist and a screenwriter. His poetry has been featured in *Chiron Review, Trailer Park Quarterly, Cultural Weekly,* and in other small presses.

Donna Hilbert's latest book is *Gravity: New and Selected Poems* (Tebot Bach, 2018). She has poems online at *A Year of Being Here, Little Eagle's RE/VERSE, Zocalo Public Square, Your Daily Poem, Serving House Journal* and monthly, as a contributing writer, at *Verse-Virtual.* Her work is widely anthologized, most recently in *Poetry of Presence* (Grayson Books). She has led workshops for both beginners and professional writers in venues as varied as a men's prison, an English public school, and literary programs including Aldeburgh Poetry and Ilkley Literature Festivals in the UK, and PEN Center USA West's Emerging Voices Rosenthal Fellows. She writes and leads private workshops in Long Beach, California, where she makes her home. www.donnahilbert.com

LeAnne Hunt (she/her) grew up in the Midwest and now lives in Orange County, California. She is a regular at the Two Idiots Peddling Poetry reading at the Ugly Mug in Orange and at the Poetry Lab workshop in Long Beach. She has poems published in *Black Napkin Press*, *Rabid Oak* and *Lullaby of Teeth: An Anthology of Southern California Poets*. She publishes a blog of writing prompts at leannehunt.com.

Tamara Madison is the author of the chapbook "The Belly Remembers," and two full-length volumes of poetry, "Wild Domestic," and "Moraine," all published by Pearl Editions. Her work has appeared in *Chiron Review, Your Daily Poem, A Year of Being Here, Nerve Cowboy, The Writer's Almanac*, and other publications.

Betsy Mars was born in Connecticut and moved a few times during childhood before landing in Southern California at age 6 (and a half). She spent two formative years in Brazil, where she attended kindergarten. She still knows the Portuguese words for cat, dog, please, and come here. Her father was a professor and her mother was a social worker, so she grew up to be a linguaphile, overly introspective, and a bleeding heart liberal. She loves to travel and write, and hang out with her adult children, friends, and animals.

Kathryn McMurray is a poet, wife, mother, and teacher living in Long Beach, California. She earned her MFA from California State University, Long Beach in 2004. Her work has appeared in *Re(Verb), The Bastille, Livewire, Pearl, Epicenter, Spork*, and *Red Rock Review*.

Aldo Moreno is a student studying Creative Writing at California State University, Long Beach. He is from Santa Clarita, California.

Holly Pelesky is a lover of spreadsheets, giant sandwiches, and handwritten letters. She holds an MFA from the University of Nebraska. She cobbles together gigs to get by, refusing to give up this writing life. She lives in Omaha with her two sons.

Natalie L. Peterkin's poetry is free verse and often explores the themes of love, lust, and loss. She is an adjunct English professor at East LA College and former poetry editor of *Pomona Valley Review*.

Wendy Rainey's poetry has been published or is forthcoming in *Trailer Park Quarterly*, *Nerve Cowboy*, *Chiron Review*, and several other journals and anthologies. Her book, *Hollywood Church: Short Stories and Poems*, was published by Vainglory Press in 2015. She is a contributing poetry editor on *Chiron Review*.

Kevin Ridgeway is from Whittier, CA. He is the author of six chapbooks of poetry. His latest book is *A Ludicrous Split* (alongside poems by Gabriel Ricard, Alien Buddha Press). Recent work has appeared or is forthcoming in *Slipstream*, *Chiron Review*, *Up the River*, *Nerve Cowboy*, *The American Journal of Poetry*, *Main Street Rag*, *Cultural Weekly*, *San Pedro River Review*, *Lummox*, *Misfit Magazine*, *Plainsongs*, and *So it Goes: The Literary Journal of the Kurt Vonnegut Memorial Library*. He lives and writes in Long Beach, CA.

A.E. Sadeghipour is a doodling Iranian-American with a Surrealist outlook. She co-founded the Berlin Diaspora Society and teaches workshops for the Women Writing Berlin Lab. She won the Sherry Debrowski Prize for Best Feminist Multi-Genre Fiction in 2009. Her work has been included in: *Matrix Feminist Literary Magazine*, *Toyon Literary Magazine*, *Hella Bitches #3*, *Seven Countries Poetry Anthology* by Arroyo Seco Press, the Berlin based magazine *The Wild Word: Dream a Little Dream*, and *Berlin and Her Places*. Preferring imagination to reality, she creates windows between the world and her reality. Check out more of her reality here: awerfjil.com

Joan Jobe Smith, founding editor of *Pearl* and *Bukowski Review*, worked 7 years as a go-go girl before graduating from CSULB and the UCI MFA Program. Since 1950 her art, poetry, prose, cooking columns, memoirs, and reviews have been published in more than 1000 literary journals, newspapers, anthologies. With her poet husband Fred Voss, she has done 7 reading tours of UK and Scotland. Her UK-published poetry collection THE POW WOW CAFE was a finalist for the 1999 Forward Prize. A Pushcart honoree with 23 poetry books (including 2 cookbooks), her award-winning work has recently appeared in *Chiron Review*, *Nerve Cowboy*, *Circe's Lament*, and the Silver Birch Poetry Series.

Kareem Tayyar's novel, *The Prince of Orange County*, was released this fall by Pelekinesis Books, and his new collection of poetry, *Immigrant Songs*, will be published by WordTech in Winter 2019. A recipient of a 2019 Wurlitzer Fellowship for Poetry, he holds a Ph.D. in American and Poetry Literature from U.C. Riverside.

Thomas R. Thomas was born in Los Angeles, CA, and grew up in the San Gabriel Valley east of LA. Currently he lives in Long Beach, CA. His latest book is *The Art of Invisibility* (Darkheart Press, 2018).

Sarah Thursday, in addition to writing poetry, co-hosted a monthly reading, ran a poetry website, and founded Sadie Girl Press. She has been published in many fine journals and anthologies, interviewed by Poetry LA, and received a 2017 Best of the Net nomination for "To the Men who told me my Love was not enough." Her poetry books are available at SadieGirlPress.com. Find and follow her to learn more on SarahThursday.com, Facebook, Twitter, or Instagram.

K. Andrew Turner writes queer, literary, and speculative prose and poetry. In 2013, he founded *East Jasmine Review* — an electronic literary journal. His full-length poetry collection *Heart, Mind, Blood, Skin* is now available from Finishing Line Press. He was a semifinalist for the 2016 Luminaire Award. You can find more at his website: www.kandrewturner.com.

Aruni Wijesinghe works as a project manager for Affinis Labs, an award-winning social innovation firm that helps clients creatively tackle complex global challenges through entrepreneurship. She holds a BA in English Literature from UCLA, an AA in Dance from Cypress College and is certified to teach English to Speakers of Other Languages (TESOL). She lives a quiet life in Orange County with her husband Jeff and their cats Jack and Josie.

Terry Ann Wright's chapbook *Mad Honey* was released in 2018 by Dancing Girl Press. Her debut chapbook *Nature Studies* was published by Sadie Girl Press in 2015; the title poem was nominated for a Pushcart Prize, her third nomination. Her poetry has appeared most recently in *The Rise Up Review, The Harpoon Review,* and *Chiron Review,* and in several anthologies.

Acknowledgments

"Blue Velvet" and "The Two Coolest Chicks" were first published in *Bottleneck Slide* (Vainglory Press, 2018).

"Paus de Deux" was previously published by *Anomaly Literary Journal*.

"Piriformis" first appeared in *Pearl* and in *The Congress of Luminous Bodies* (Aortic Books, 2013). Earlier versions of "At Parties" and "Ingénue" were published in *The Green Season* (World Parade Books, 2011).

"Sharcas" was previously published in *Like a Girl: Perspectives on Feminine Identity* (Lucid Moose Lit, 2015) and in *Heart, Mind, Blood, Skin* (Finishing Line Press, 2018).

www.ingramcontent.com/pod-product-compliance
Lightning Source LLC
Chambersburg PA
CBHW071624040426
42452CB00009B/1479